RAF, Dominion & Allied Squadrons at War:
Study, History and Statistics

Compiled by
Phil H. Listemann

Drawings by Claveworks Classics

Preface

The purpose of this study is to provide aviation historians and enthusiasts with a range of information relative to each of the Commonwealth squadrons that saw combat during World War II. Each record will comprise a short history, complete with illustrations and artwork, and accompanied by the following appendices:

Appendix I: Squadron Commanders and Flight Commanders
Appendix II: Major awards
Appendix III: Operational diary (number of sorties per month)
Appendix IV: Victory list
Appendix V: Aircraft losses on operations
Appendix VI: Aircraft losses in accidents
Appendix VII: Aircraft Serial numbers matching with individual letters (including mission totals for multi-engine aircraft)
Appendix VIII: Nominal roll (Captains only for bomber and seaplane units)
Appendix IX: Roll of Honour

Individual files will be constantly updated, when any fresh information comes to light. Additional information will be available for download, at no charge, on each squadron's site at:

Glossary of Terms

Ranks

AC: Aircraftman
G/C: Group Captain
W/C: Wing Commander
S/L: Squadron Leader
F/L: Flight Lieutenant
F/O: Flying Officer
P/O: Pilot Officer
W/O: Warrant Officer
F/Sgt: Flight Sergeant
Sgt: Sergeant
Cpl: Corporal
LAC: Leading Aircraftman

Other

AAF: Auxiliary Air Force
CO: Commanding Officer
DFC: Distinguished Flying Cross
DFM: Distinguished Flying Medal
DSO: Distinguished Service Order
Eva.: Evaded
Inj.: Injured
ORB: Operational Record Book
OTU: Operational Training Unit
PAF: Polish Air Force
PoW: Prisoner of War
RAF: Royal Air Force
RAAF: Royal Australian Air Force
RCAF: Royal Canadian Air Force
RNZAF: Royal New Zealand Air Force
SAAF: South African Air Force
Sqn: Squadron
TOC: Taken on charge
†: Killed

No.133 (Eagle) Squadron 1941-1942

ISBN: 978-2918590-73-6

Contributors & Acknowledgments:
Paul Sortehaug.

Copyright

© 2010 Philedition - Phil Listemann
Revised 2012, 2015

All right reserved. No part of this book may be reproduced, stored in a retrieval system or transmitted in any form by any means, electronic, mechanical, photocopying, recording or otherwise, without prior permission of the author.

Cover: Squadron Leader Eric H. Thomas is taxiing to lead another mission on his aircraft BM263/MD-A.

Main Equipment

Hurricane II	Aug.41 - Dec.41
Spitfire II	Oct.41 - Jan.42
Spitfire V	Jan.42 - Sep.42
Spitfire IX	Aug.42 - Sep.42

Squadron Code Letters:

MD

Squadron History

The continuous flow of Americans enlisting in either the RAF or RCAF, saw the formation of a third fighter squadron, No.133 Squadron, following, just 10 weeks after, the formation of the second 'Eagle' Squadron, No.121. Formed at Colstishall on **1 August 1941**, the training began, on Hurricane Mk.IIs at once, under the guidance of a British CO, S/L G.A. Brown, formerly of No.71 Squadron, the first 'Eagle' Squadron. He was supported initially by his two Flight Commanders, also British, although they were soon replaced by experienced American 'Eagle' pilots.

At the end of September the squadron became operational, performing its first two sorties on the 29th. The Hurricanes did not last too long with the arrival of the first Spitfire Mk.IIs coming in October. As events unfolded No.133 Squadron did not have a happy introduction and was hit by bad luck during the 1941 autumn, losing eight pilots, seven of whom were killed in flying accidents in just a couple of weeks. Four of these casualties took place during a cross-country flight to the Isle of Man on the 8th October. Nevertheless the squadron continued to fly over the East Coast on convoy patrols and sector recces and was refurbished with Spifire Mk.Vs in January 1942. Their first claim came on 5 February when, during the course of a convoy patrol, two Do 217's were encountered, one being destroyed with another squadron and the other damaged.

During April the squadron began to take part in offensive Wing sweeps, and towards the end of the month was allocated 'Fighter Night' duties in defence of York, albeit with little success. A move to Biggin Hill in May gave the Americans the opportunity they were seeking, and from then on they were heavily engaged in Wing sweeps and bomber escorts. On 4 June the squadron provided cover to a commando raid between Boulogne and Le Touquet, and in July began *Rhubarb* sorties. That same month saw a change in leadership, with an American taking over command. The Dieppe raid of 19 August 1942, led by the charismatic F/L Don' Blakeslee, was the last major action the squadron took part in, undertaking four patrols over the raid area. These netted 6 enemy aircraft destroyed, 2 probables and 8 damaged for no loss, two of the confirmed going to Pilot Officer Don Gentile. After briefly being rested the unit came back to the front line, in September 1942, with Fighter Command's latest mount, the Spitfire Mk.IX. It therefore became one the first squadrons to use it on operations. However, that same month, it was once again hit by misfortune losing 12 aircraft and 11 pilots, killed or taken prisoner, during an operation over the Continent on the 26th. This was one of the heaviest losses of the war sustained by a single fighter squadron in Fighter Command, and a severe blow for the Command itself, which was not over endowed with this highly valued Spitfire model.

Three days later, **29 September 1942**, exactly a year after being declared operational and only just after having received an urgent influx of personnel and Spitfire Mk.Vs, to replace the recent losses, No.133 Squadron was incorporated into the U.S. Army Air Corps as 336th Fighter Squadron. Its statistics in Fighter Command were 22.5 aircraft destroyed or probably destroyed, during the course of nearly 2,000 sorties, for the loss of 35 pilots, killed or taken prisoner.

[1] *No.133 Sqn was first formed in March 1918 and was disbanded in July the same year.*

Squadron Bases

Coltishall	31.07.41 - 15.08.41	Lympne	30.06.42 - 12.07.42
Duxford	15.08.41 - 28.09.41	Biggin Hill	12.07.42 - 31.07.42
Collyweston	28.09.41 - 03.10.41	Gravesend	31.07.42 - 17.08.42
Fowlmere	03.10.41 - 08.10.41	Lympne	17.08.42 - 22.08.42
Eglinton	08.10.41 - 02.01.42	Martlesham Heath	22.08.42 - 31.08.42
Kirton-in-Lindsey	02.01.42 - 03.05.42	Biggin Hill	31.08.42 - 23.09.42
Biggin Hill	03.05.42 - 30.06.42	Great Sampford	23.09.42 - 29.09.42

No.133 (Eagle) Squadron

Recruting Pilots

Shoulder badge of American volunteers serving one of the Eagle Squadrons.

Shoulder badge of American volunteers for officers. The Eagle pilots were actually a tiny part of the Americans who served the RAF and RCAF during the war.

From the very beginning of the war in Europe Americans, at all levels, took an interest, realising that, sooner or later, they would be involved. Creating a fighter squadron comprising American volunteers quickly took root in certain minds, including Charles Sweeny's, an ex-serviceman of the French Foreign Legion during World War One. He was one who had been inspired by the exploits of the famous Lafayette squadron, manned by Americans, and the status it held, all of which had been portrayed by the media of that time.

He established a network, allowing interested Americans to cross the Atlantic, to support France, although French enthusiasm on this occasion was not so positive. Compounding Sweeny's problems was a Congress Neutrality Act, voted in 1935 and revised and reinforced many times thereafter, making the recruiting of American volunteers for fighting in Foreign countries very difficult indeed. The US authorities closely monitored activity of this nature and would not facilitate any enlistment. Volunteers, or for that matter anyone suspected as being one, would be detained at the Canadian border, this situation existing right up until the fall of France in June 1940. As a result volunteers arrived too late, and the French overwhelmed by their own situation had little to offer them. Consequently the vast majority disappeared amid the upheaval, either killed or made prisoners, while others returned to the USA by their own means. Only five of the original volunteers are known to have arrived in Great Britain.

Thereafter the situation changed and American authorities became more accommodating. At the same time the number of volunteers increased, since many were aware that the USA was readying to enter the war. The Knight Committee, from the name of its founder, was set up and this organisation would be responsible for the bulk of American recruitment, starting in the spring of 1940. In August 1941 this committee became the Canadian Aviation Bureau, before being disbanded late in 1942. Some 250 American pilots would serve with three American fighter units - the Eagle Squadrons - formed in the RAF between 1940 and 1942. These though were only a fraction of the hundreds, who passed through the committee, to enrol in the RAF or the RCAF, and fight under the RAF umbrella in Europe, the Middle East and the Far East. Their motives were varied, but the majority simply sought adventure. Their aspirations were to become pilots but they had been refused entry into their own country's air arms, on educational, competency or medical grounds. Both the RCAF and the RAF (Royal Air Force Volunteer Reserve - RAFVR) provided viable alternatives, and the prospect of flying a Spitfire, by then the best Allied fighter, only added to reinforce their desire to join up.

The American pilots, in particular those that served with the Eagle Squadrons, were to benefit from certain privileges. Most were not required to pledge allegiance to the King, upon their engagement, and thus were able to maintain their American citizenship. Additionally, it was understood that, those passed by the Knight Committee would be commissioned at the end of their training, as opposed to the majority of those who joined the RCAF, who graduated as Non-Commissioned Officers. This disparity was to create problems when the integration of these pilots into the Army Air Force took place.

Transfer to the AAF

The Transfer of personnel to the AAF, a natural outcome, was not so simple for numerous reasons. Firstly, the RAF had put a considerable investment into their training, and they were fully operational, and doing a fine job, when America entered the war in December 1941. The British simply were not in a hurry to disband the three American fighter squadrons. The pilots themselves had signed up with the RAFVR, that is, until the end of the war, and adding to English woes, they now faced war on a new front with Japan. Integration into the AAF meant that the pilots trained by the RAF would, sooner or later, come into contact with countrymen trained in American schools, and this would not be to everyone's satisfaction. At certain levels 'Eagle' flyers had been subjected to a British influence, not always well embraced by Americans.

Rank equivalence also posed problems. The AAF did not have anyone below the base rank of Second Lieutenant as a pilot. NCOs transferring from the RCAF would automatically have to become Second Lieutenants. The situation involving officers was relatively straight forward - they would acquire the comparative rank. There was also debate about how these transferees should be utilised. 8th Air Force officials of rank felt that it would be logical to divide these pilots amongst AAF units arriving in England, where their solid experience would be of some benefit.

Others were of the opinion that the three Eagle squadrons, having established a fine reputation and not wishing to separate, should be forged into a specific unit - the 4th Fighter Group. In effect this was what happened in September of 1942. However some pilots chose to remain in the RAF, out of loyalty and feeling the change would not be in their best interests.

As for the 4th FG it was to keep its unique identity for the early months of it's existence, but by the summer of 1943, due to losses and manpower turnover, it would become an American Fighter Group, falling in line with all the others.

For those who choose to integrate into the AAF, it was not immediately apparent whether they had made the correct choice or not. While they gained a pay increase and access to an array of typically American luxuries, they lost an element of prestige with the British population who held them in high regard - they were considered to be a cut above the average American. There was also the loss of spirit and friendship, very present within the British units, which became more obvious with the arrival of American pilots coming from the USA, replacing those who were lost or had left.

The pilots of the Eagle Squadrons were special, being volunteers in a British war that was not theirs and, for political reasons, they had been courted by and received a great deal of press. Once integration into the AAF had taken place, this became something of a burden. The AAF moved quickly to tone down their amount of press coverage so that they would become less conspicuous, for both morale and political reasons.

Shoulder badge of American volunteers serving the RCAF.

Variant of shoulder badge for American volunteers.

APPENDIX I
Squadron and Flight Commanders

Rank and Name	SN	Origin	Dates
S/L George A. **Brown**	RAF No.39851	RAF	01.08.41 - 27.11.41
S/L Eric H. **Thomas**	RAF No.39138	RAF	27.11.41 - 01.08.42
F/L Donald J.M. **Blakeslee** (Temp.)	Can./J.4551	(US)/RCAF	01.08.42 - 01.09.42
S/L Caroll W. **McColpin**	RAF No.61926	(US)/RAF	01.09.42 - 29.09.42

A Flight

Rank and Name	SN	Origin	Dates
F/L Hugh A.S. **Johnstone**	RAF No.88723	RAF	27.08.41 - 07.03.42
F/L Vivian E. **Watkins**	RAF No.64868	(US)/RAF	07.03.42 - 19.04.42
F/L Colin C. **King** (†)	RAF No.100521	(US)/RAF	19.04.42 - 31.07.42
F/L Edward G. **Brettel** (PoW)	RAF No.61053	RAF	07.08.42 - 26.09.42

B Flight

Rank and Name	SN	Origin	Dates
F/L George W. **Scott**	RAF No.62257	RAF	18.08.41 - 02.09.41
F/L Andrew B. **Mamedoff** (†)	RAF No.81621	(US)/RAF	02.09.41 - 08.10.41
F/L Charles E. **Bateman**	RAF No.83703	(US)/RAF	23.10.41 - 23.01.42
F/L Caroll W. **McColpin**	RAF No.61926	(US)/RAF	23.01.42 - 01.05.42
F/L Donald J.M. **Blakeslee**	Can./J.4551	(US)/RCAF	01.05.42 - 29.09.42

APPENDIX II
Major Awards

DSO: -

DFC: 3
William Henry **Baker** (No.108626 - RAF), USA
Donald James Matthew **Blakeslee** (Can./J.4551 - RCAF), USA
Edward Gordon **Brettell** (No.61053 - RAF)

DFM: -

APPENDIX III
OPERATIONAL DIARY - NUMBER OF SORTIES PER MONTH

Date	Month	Total	Date	Month	Total
Sep.41	8	8	Jun.42	327	1,573
Oct.41	72	80	Jul.42	178	1,751
Nov.41	51	131	Aug.42	191	1,942
Dec.41	70	201	Sep.42	36	1,978
Jan.42	60	261			
Feb.42	306	567	**Grand Total**	1,978	1,978
Mar.42	198	765			
Avr.42	219	984			
May.42	262	1,246			

Extracted from AIR27/945

APPENDIX IV
VICTORY LIST
CONFIRMED (C) AND PROBABLE (P) CLAIMS

Date	Pilot	SN	Origin	Type	Serial	Code	Nb	Cat.
			SPITFIRE V					
05.02.42	F/L Hugh A.S. Johnstone	RAF No.88723	RAF	Do217	P8195		0.25	C
	P/O Marion A. Jackson	RAF No.100519	(US)/RAF		P9397		0.25	C
Shared with two No.253 Sqn pilots, P/O P. Landers and Sgt J.C. Tate.								
26.04.42	F/L Caroll W. McColpin	RAF No.61926	(US)/RAF	Fw190	BM300		1.0	C
27.04.42	P/O Robert L. Pewitt	RAF No.100528	(US)/RAF	Fw190	BL988		1.0	P
	P/O William H. Baker	RAF No.108826	(US)/RAF	Fw190	BL492		1.0	P
17.05.42	P/O Moran S. Morris	RAF No.102052	(US)/RAF	Bf109	BL996		1.0	P
	F/L Caroll W. McColpin	RAF No.61926	(US)/RAF	Bf109	BM300		1.0	C
	F/L Caroll W. McColpin	RAF No.61926	(US)/RAF	Bf109	BM300		1.0	P
19.05.42	P/O Moran S. Morris	RAF No.105052	(US)/RAF	Bf109	BL996		1.0	C
	F/Sgt Carter W. Harp	Can./R.74201	(US)/RCAF	Bf109	BL982		2.0	C
05.06.42	S/L Eric H. Thomas	RAF No.39138	RAF	Bf109	BM263	MD-A	1.0	P
31.07.42	P/O William H. Baker	RAF No.108826	(US)/RAF	Fw190	EN924		1.0	C
	P/O Edwin D. Taylor	RAF No.102053	(US)/RAF	Fw190	BM591		1.0	C
18.08.42	F/L Donald J.M. Blakeslee	Can./J.4551	(US)/RCAF	Bf109	EN951	MD-U	1.0	C
19.08.42	F/Sgt Richard L. Alexander	Can./R.67881	(US)/RCAF	Fw190	BL773		1.0	P
	F/L Donald J.M. Blakeslee	Can./J.4551	(US)/RCAF	Fw190	EN951	MD-U	1.0	P
	P/O William H. Baker	RAF No.108826	(US)/RAF	Fw190	EN834		1.0	C
	F/L Edward G. Bretell	RAF No.61053	RAF	Fw190	AD237		1.0	C
	F/L Donald J.M. Blakeslee	Can./J.4551	(US)/RCAF	Do217	EN951	MD-U	1.0	C
	P/O Dominic S. Gentile	RAF No.112302	(US)/RAF	Fw190	BM530		1.0	C
				Ju88	BM530		1.0	C
	F/Sgt Richard L. Alexander	Can./R.67881	(US)/RCAF	Do217	AB910		1.0	C

SPITFIRE IX

07.09.42	P/O William H. BAKER	RAF No.108826	(US)/RAF	Fw190	BS137	MD-D	1.0	P

Total: 22.5
Aircraft damaged: 18.5

APPENDIX V
AIRCRAFT LOST ON OPERATIONS

Date	Pilot	S/N	Origin	Serial	Code	Mark	Fate

HURRICANE

23.10.41	P/O George R. BRUCE	RAF No.67580	(US)/RAF	Z3649		IIB	†

Took off at 10.40 with Sgt Carter Harp (RCAF) for a convoy patrol. Returning from base, he made an unauthorised low pass over the airfield, struck a tree, and crashed. P/O Bruce was a Canadian-born American, who had served with the squadron since July.
<u>Note on the aircraft</u> : TOC No.27 MU 11.06.41. Issued to No.133 Sqn 30.09.41 from No.401(RCAF) Sqn.

SPITFIRE

16.03.42	P/O Hugh C. BROWN	RAF No.103467	(US)/RAF	X4353		VA	†

Took off at 08.25 with F/Sgt Carter Harp (RCAF) for a weather test over the Channel to establish whether convoy patrols could be safely conducted. When at a spot 15 m E. of Mablethorpe, F/Sgt Harp called up P/O Brown telling him that he was going to climb as visibility was practically nil. There was no answer and it was assumed that P/O Brown crashed into the sea. Canadian-born American who had served in the squadron since October 1941.
<u>Note on the aircraft</u> : Built as a Mk.I; TOC No.24 MU 07.09.40. Served with Nos.19, 65, 145, 118, 66 and 501 Sqns before being converted to a Mk.VA in Autumn 1941. Issued to No.133 Sqn 20.12.41 from 145 Sqn and having served previously with No.603 Sqn.

27.04.42	F/Sgt Walter C. WICKER	CAN./R.74415	(US)/RCAF	BM264		VB	†

Took off with 17 others for CIRCUS 142 at 18.00, No.133 Sqn being the top squadron of the formation comprising Nos.616 and 412 (RCAF) Sqns. On reaching Ostend (Belgium), about 30 Fw190s were seen above at 21,000 feet. No.133 Sqn was soon engaged and F/Sgt Wicker was heard over the radio to say that he had been hit. He was reported missing and his body was washed up at Dover two days later. An American from Illinois who had been in the Squadron four months.
<u>Note on the aircraft</u> : TOC No.5 MU 23.03.42. Presentation aircraft 'SHETLANDER', issued to No.133 Sqn 12.04.42.

29.04.42	P/O Eric DOORLY	RAF No.101458	(US)/RAF	BL995	MD-G	VB	-

Took off with S/L Thomas for a night patrol at 02.30 Intercepted and engaged a Do217 damaging it in the process. Was hit in the glycol tank by return fire. Temperature rose to 140°C and engine finally cut. Doorly, from New Jersey, baled out safely. See also 06.09.42 entry.
<u>Note on the aircraft</u> : TOC No.12 MU 19.02.42, issued to No.133 Sqn 13.04.42 from 601 Sqn.

19.05.42   P/O Robert L. **PEWITT**   RAF No.100528   (US)/RAF   **BL988**   VB   †

Took off for a RODEO over Fécamp-Le Tréport (France) with 11 others at 14.25. Hit and severely damaged by enemy fighters and crashed into sea off Beachy Head. Rescued but died of head injuries before being admitted to hospital. American from Texas, who had served in the squadron since September 1941.

<u>Note on the aircraft</u> : TOC No.12 MU 26.02.42, issued to No.133 Sqn 07.04.42 from 601 Sqn.

         P/O David R. **FLORANCE**   CAN./J.15193   (US)/RCAF   **AD502**   VB   †

Took off for a Rodeo over Fécamp-Le Tréport (France) with 11 others at 14.25. Shot down by enemy fighters. A Canadian-born American who was a founder member of the Squadron.

<u>Note on the aircraft</u> : TOC No.8 MU 19.10.41, issued to No.133 Sqn 04.05.42 from No.332 (Norwegian) Sqn. Served also with Nos.603 Sqn.

31.05.42   P/O William K. **FORD**   RAF No.111238   (US)/RAF   **BL961**   VB   †

Took off at 18.45 with 11 others for a sweep over Dieppe - Fécamp (France). Encountered and engaged Fw190s. P/O Ford did not return being presumed shot down by enemy fighters. An American from Texas who had served with the squadron for two months.

<u>Note on the aircraft</u> : TOC No.12 MU 19.02.42, issued to No.133 Sqn 30.04.42 from 601 Sqn.

         P/O Moran S. **MORRIS**   RAF No.102052   (US)/RAF   **BL996**   VB   †

Took off at 18.45 with 11 others for a sweep over Dieppe - Fécamp (France). Encountered and engaged Fw190s. P/O Morris did not return and was presumed shot down by enemy fighters. An American from Oklahoma who had served with the Squadron for nearly six months.

<u>Note on the aircraft</u> : TOC No.39 MU 22.02.42, issued to No.133 Sqn 07.04.42. Previously served with Nos.601, 133, 402 (RCAF) and 308 (Polish) Sqns.

05.06.42   P/O Fletcher **HANCOCK**   RAF No.112280   (US)/RAF   **BM260**   MD-C   VB   †

Took off with 12 others at 15.00 for a diversionary sweep over Abbeville (France), with No.72 Sqn, while Bostons bombed Le Havre. Engaged Fw190s and P/O Hancock was shot down near Abeville (France). He was last seen in dogfight over the French coast at Cayeux. American from California, who had served in the Squadron for a little more than two months.

<u>Note on the aircraft</u> : TOC No.20 MU 25.03.42. Presentation aircraft 'POPEYE'S PAL'. Issued to No.133 Sqn 12.04.42.

20.06.42   P/O William A. **ARENDS**   RAF No.112280   (US)/RAF   **EP168**   VB   †

Took off with 12 others at 14.55 for a diversionary sweep to Hardelot -St.Omer (France), while Bostons bombed Le Havre. Bounced by Fw190s in target area. American from North Dakota, who had served with the squadron since March.

<u>Note on the aircraft</u> : TOC No.9 MU 27.05.42, issued to No.133 Sqn 13.06.42.

31.07.42   F/L Colin C. **KING**   RAF No.100521   (US)/RAF   **BL938**   VB   †

Took off at 14.20 with 12 others on CIRCUS 201 (Abbeville aerodrome). Flying with Nos.72 and 65 Sqns, No.133 Sqn was positioned at the bottom of the formation at 8,000 ft. Just before crossing the French coast, on the return flight, the squadron was intercepted by Fw190s, and F/L King was shot down off Pas de Calais (France). From Missouri and aged 33 pilot was well above the age of the average fighter pilot. He had served in the squadron since August 1941 and held the post of 'A' Flight Commander.

<u>Note on the aircraft</u> : TOC No.9 MU 22.02.42, issued to No.133 Sqn 08.04.42 from No.601 Sqn.

         P/O Carter W. **HARP**   CAN./J.15389   (US)/RCAF   **BL982**   VB   †

Took off at 14.20 with 12 others on CIRCUS 201 (Abbeville aerodrome). As above. Shot down by FW190s off Boulogne (France). At 33 pilot was well above the age of the average fighter pilot. From Alabama he had served with the squadron since October 1941.

<u>Note on the aircraft</u> : TOC No.39 MU 22.02.42, issued to No.133 Sqn 12.04.42 from No.601 Sqn.

| | F/Sgt Grant E. **Eichar** | Can./R.83097 | (US)/RCAF | **BM646** | | VB | † |

Took off at 14.20 with 12 others on CIRCUS 201 (Abbeville aerodrome). As above. Shot down by Fw190s near Abbeville (France). American from Iowa who had served with the squadron since February. Although commissioned (J.15650), Eichar had yet to receive notification.
Note on the aircraft : TOC No.9 MU 09.05.42, issued to No.133 Sqn 13.06.42.

| **04.09.42** | P/O Ernest D. **Beaty** | RAF No.116468 | (US)/RAF | **BS297** | | IXB | - |

Took off at 14.15 to orbit Canterbury at 25,000 ft. with P/O Len Ryerson. While climbing they were informed that an unidentified aircraft was flying above at 35,000 ft. They continued to climb and a Ju86 was seen flying S.W. over North Foreland, and in turn commenced climbing. P/O Beaty manoeuvred into line astern and slightly below and fired a short burst of cannon and machine gun observing strikes on its underside. The pair reached 40,000 ft and the Ju86 continued flying straight and still climbing. At that moment P/O Beaty's engine gave out and he began a descent. However at 20,000 ft the engine commenced smoking and pilot was forced to bale out. His aircraft crashed in sea off Manston. American from New York he had been with the squadron since April. Later in September he transferred to the USAAF and ended the war with one confirmed victory.
Note on the aircraft : TOC 13.08.42, issued to No.133 Sqn 16.08.42.

| **06.09.42** | P/O Dick D. **Gudmundsen** | RAF No.112295 | (US)/RAF | **BS292** | | IXB | † |

Took off at 16.55 with 11 others on a CIRCUS, escorting B-17s to Rouen. During return flight, for unknown reasons, the B-17s began to fire at the air cover, forcing the Spitfires to dive down to sea-level. P/O Gudmundsen did not return. American from Idaho who had been in the squadron less than three months.
Note on the aircraft : TOC 09.08.42, issued to No.133 Sqn 11.08.42.

| | F/O Eric **Doorly** | RAF No.101458 | (US)/RAF | **BS276** | | IXB | Eva. |

Took off at 16.55 with 11 others on a CIRCUS, escorting B-17s to Rouen. As above. Returned to the UK in April 1943 and transferred to the USAAF. Served in Europe, ending the war with three German aircraft destroyed. (See also 29.04.42 entry).
Note on the aircraft : Built as Mk.V but converted to Mk.IX on the production line. TOC 07.08.42, issued to No.133 Sqn 12.08.42.

| **26.09.42** | F/L Edward G. **Brettel** | RAF No.61053 | RAF | **BS313** | MD-A | IXB | PoW |

Took off at 16.00 leading the Squadron on a CIRCUS, escorting B-17s to Morlaix. 'A' Flight Commander and lost as a result of adverse weather conditions. Later reported PoW at Stalag Luft III. Gordon (as he was better known) served previously with No.92 Sqn. Was one of the 76 escapees during the 'Great Escape' and also one of those who was recaptured and shot by the Gestapo.
Note on the aircraft : TOC 05.09.42, issued to No.133 Sqn 08.09.42.

| | F/L Marion E. **Jackson** | RAF No.100519 | (US)/RAF | **BS279** | | IXB | PoW |

Took off at 16.00 with twelve others on a CIRCUS to Morlaix. Lost as a result of adverse weather conditions. An American from Texas who had served with the squadron since August 1941. Although he had transferred to the USAAF on 16 September 1942 it is thought he was still in RAF uniform as he was later reported as an RAF officer being held PoW in Stalag Luft III.
Note on the aircraft : Built as Mk.V but converted to Mk.IX on the production line. TOC 16.08.42, issued to No.133 Sqn 17.08.42.

| | F/O George B. **Sperry** | RAF No.100533 | (US)/RAF | **BR638** | | IXB | PoW |

Took off at 16.00 with twelve others on a CIRCUS to Morlaix. Lost as a result of adverse weather conditions. An American from California who had been with the squadron since July 1941. Although he had transferred to the USAAF on 16 September 1942 it is thought he was still in RAF uniform as he was later reported as an RAF officer being held PoW in Stalag Luft III.
Note on the aircraft : Built as Mk.V but converted to Mk.IX on the production line. TOC 05.08.42, issued to No.133 Sqn 10.08.42.

| | P/O Charles A. **Cook** | RAF No.103476 | (US)/RAF | **BR640** | MD-V | IXB | PoW |

Took off at 16.00 with twelve others on a CIRCUS to Morlaix. Lost as a result of adverse weather conditions. An American from

California who had served with the squadron since October 1941. Although he had transferred to the USAAF on 15 September 1942 it is thought he was still in RAF uniform as he was later reported as an RAF officer being held PoW in Stalag Luft III.

<u>Note on the aircraft</u> : Built as Mk.V but converted to Mk.IX on the production line. TOC 14.08.42, issued to No.133 Sqn 16.08.42.

    P/O George H. **Middleton**   RAF No.112286   (US)/RAF   **BS301**   IXB   **PoW**

Took off at 16.00 with twelve others on a CIRCUS to Morlaix. Lost as a result of adverse weather conditions. An American from Iowa who had been in the squadron since June. Previously had served with No.121 (Eagle) Sqn Although he had transferred to the USAAF on 16 September 1942 it is thought he was still in RAF uniform as he was later reported as an RAF officer being held PoW in Stalag Luft III.

<u>Note on the aircraft</u> : TOC 18.08.42, issued to No.133 Sqn 19.08.42.

    P/O Gilbert G. **Wright**   RAF No.112286   (US)/RAF   **BS138**   IXB   **PoW**

Took off at 16.00 with twelve others on a CIRCUS to Morlaix. Lost as a result of adverse weather conditions. An American from Pennsylvania who had served with the squadron less than two months. Although he had transferred to the USAAF on 16 September 1942 it is thought he was still in RAF uniform as he was later reported as an RAF officer being held PoW in Stalag Luft III.

<u>Note on the aircraft</u> : TOC 08.08.42, issued to No.133 Sqn 11.08.42.

    P/O Gene P. **Neville**   RAF No.115120   (US)/RAF   **BS140**   IXB   †

Took off at 16.00 with twelve others for a CIRCUS mission to Morlaix. Lost to adverse weather. An American from Oklahoma who had served in the squadron less than two months. Although he had transferred to the USAAF the previous day it is thought he was still in RAF uniform. He is also recorded as an USAAF loss with service number O-885129.

<u>Note on the aircraft</u> : TOC 14.08.42, issued to No.133 Sqn 17.08.42.

    P/O Leonard T. **Ryerson**   RAF No.112285   (US)/RAF   **BS275**   IXB   †

Took off at 16.00 with twelve others on a CIRCUS to Morlaix. Lost as a result of adverse weather conditions. An American from New Hampshire who had served in the squadron since May. Although he had transferred to the USAAF on 16 September 1942 it is thought he was still in RAF uniform. He is also recorded an an USAAF loss with service number O-885137.

<u>Note on the aircraft</u> : Built as Mk.V but converted to Mk.IX on the production line. TOC 09.08.42 issued to No.133 Sqn 12.08.42.

    F/O William H. **Baker** Jr.   RAF No.108626   (US)/RAF   **BS446**   IXB   †

Took off at 16.00 with twelve others on a CIRCUS to Morlaix. Lost as a result of adverse weather conditions. An American from Texas who had served in the squadron since December 1941. Although he had transferred to the USAAF on 16 September 1942 it is thought he was still in RAF uniform. He is also recorded an USAAF loss with service number O-885113.

<u>Note on the aircraft</u> : TOC 11.09.42, issued to No.133 Sqn 13.09.42.

    P/O Dennis D. **Smith**   RAF No.116464   (US)/RAF   **BS294**   MD-I   IXB   †

Took off at 16.00 with twelve others on a Circus to Morlaix. Lost as a result of adverse weather conditions. An American from Oklahoma who had served in the squadron since June. Although he had transferred to the USAAF on 16 September 1942 it is thought he was still in RAF uniform. He is also recorded an USAAF loss with service number O-885128.

<u>Note on the aircraft</u> : TOC 11.08.42, issued to No.133 Sqn 13.08.42.

    P/O Robert E. **Smith**   RAF No.116463   (US)/RAF   **BS447**   IXB   **Eva.**

Took off at 16.00 with twelve others on a CIRCUS to Morlaix. Lost as a result of adverse weather conditions. An American from Maryland who had served in the squadron since June. Although he had transferred to the USAAF on 16 September 1942 it is thought he was still in RAF uniform. He managed to evade capture with the French underground and returned to the UK in January 1943 and eventually sent back to the USA.

<u>Note on the aircraft</u> : TOC 11.09.42, issued to No.133 Sqn 13.09.42.

Total: 27

APPENDIX VI
Aircraft Lost in Accidents

Hurricane

27.09.41   P/O Walter G. **Soares**   RAF No.100532   (US)/RAF   **Z3335**   MD-B   IIB   †
Collided with Charles Barrel's aircraft while turning onto final approach at Dufford and crashed at Anton Hill. Soares, an American from California, had arrived at the squadron only a month earlier direct from No.56 OTU.
Note on the aircraft : TOC No.15 MU 08.05.41, issued to No.133 Sqn 25.08.41 from No.71(Eagle)Sqn.

         P/O Charles S. **Barrell**   RAF No.102519   (US)/RAF   **Z3828**   MD-F   IIB   †
Collided with Walter Soares' aircraft while turning onto final approach at Dufford and crashed at Anton Hill. Barrell, an American from Massachussetts, had arrived at the squadron just four days earlier direct from an OTU.
Note on the aircraft : TOC No.29 MU 21.06.41, issued to No.133 Sqn 25.08.41 from No.71(Eagle)Sqn.

08.10.41   F/L Andrew B. **Mamedoff**   RAF No.81621   (US)/RAF   **Z3781**   MD-U   IIB   †
Crashed Ballaskeig Moor, near Ramsey, Isle of Man, during a ferry flight to Eglington, because of bad weather. Mamedoff, an American from Connecticut, was 'B' Flight Commander, and had been a founder member of the first Eagle Squadron, No.71. Also a Battle of Britain veteran who had flown with No.609 Squadron.
Note on the aircraft : TOC No.29 MU 17.06.41, issued to No.133 Sqn 25.08.41 from No.71 (Eagle)Sqn.

         P/O William J. **White**   RAF No.100535   (US)/RAF   **Z3457**   MD-Y   IIB   †
Crashed Ballaskeig Moor, near Ramsey, Isle of Man, during a ferry flight to Eglington, because of bad weather. An American from Illinois, White had been posted to the squadron, from No.56 OTU, in August.
Note on the aircraft : TOC No.44 MU 08.05.41, issued to No.133 Sqn 25.08.41 from No.71(Eagle)Sqn.

         P/O Roy N. **Stout** Jr.   RAF No.100531   (US)/RAF   **Z3253**   IIB   †
Crashed Snaefell, NW of Laxey, Isle of Man, during a ferry flight to Eglington, because of bad weather. Stout, an American from Missouri, had joined the squadron on 1 September from No.56 OTU.
Note on the aircraft : TOC No.19 MU 24.04.41, issued to No.133 Sqn 26.08.41 from No.32 Sqn.

         P/O Hugh H. **McCall**   RAF No.67583   (US)/RAF   **Z3677**   IIB   †
Crashed North Laxey, near Ramsey, Isle of Man, during a ferry flight to Eglington, because of bad weather. McCall an American from Minnesota, was a founder member of the squadron.
Note on the aircraft : TOC No.51 MU 25.06.41, issued to No.133 Sqn 25.08.41. Served previously with No.71 (Eagle) Sqn.

27.10.41   P/O James G. **Coxetter**   RAF No.104392   (US)/RAF   **Z3182**   IIB   †
Crashed during a training flight at Roslarkin, Ulster, probably due to a loss of control. Pilot baled out but was too low for his parachute to open and was killed. An American from Florida who had been with the squadron less than a month.
Note on the aircraft : TOC No.51 MU 09.04.41, issued to No.133 Sqn 25.08.41 from No.71(Eagle)Sqn.

Spitfire

30.11.41 P/O Roland L. **Wolfe** RAF No.102518 (US)/RAF **P8074** IIA **Int.**

Got lost in bad weather due to radio failure, ran out of fuel and baled out over the Irish Free State, being interned. An American from Arkansas, who had joined the squadron in August. Escaped towards the end of 1943, and transferred to the USAAF in November of that year.

Note on the aircraft : TOC No.37 MU 24.02.41. Presentation aircraft 'GARFIELD WESTON I'. Issued to No.133 Sqn 28.10.41, having served previously with Nos.222 & 501 Sqns.

05.02.42 F/Sgt Frederick C. **Austin** Can./R.58580 (US)/RCAF **W3379** VA -

Hit snowdrift on take off for a training flight and overturned, Kirton-in-Lindsey. American from California, Fred Austin was serving the squadron since December and was posted to No.121 Sqn at the end of March with which he was killed in action on 17.04.42.

Note on the aircraft : TOC No.33 MU 15.06.41. Issued to No.133 Sqn 02.01.42, having served previously with Nos.603, 145, 134 and 133 Sqns.

03.04.42 P/O Samuel F. **Whedon** RAF No.101462 (US)/RAF **P8438** VA †

Collided with P8595 during a training flight and abandoned near Epworth, Lincs. A strong gust of wind caught his parachute, causing Whedon to lose his footing, fall backwards, and fatally strike his head on a rock. An American from Wisconsin, who had served with the squadron since September 1941.

Note on the aircraft : Built as a Mk.II, TOC No.33 MU 18.04.41. Presentation aircraft 'CARDIFF III'. Served briefly with No.616 Sqn before being converted to a Mk.VA. Served with Nos.145 & 134 Sqns before to be issued to No.133 Sqn 29.12.41.

P/O William A. **Arends** RAF No.112280 (US)/RAF **P8595** VA -

Collided with P8438 during a training flight and abandoned near Epworth, Lincs. Arends had been in the squadron for three weeks. He was killed two months later in action (see operational losses).

Note on the aircraft : Built as a Mk.II, TOC No.6 MU 07.06.41. Presentation aircraft 'MIDDELBERG'. Served briefly with No.66 Sqn before being damaged in combat 24.08.41. Repaired and converted to Mk.VA and issued to No.133 Sqn 01.04.42.

25.04.42 Sgt Grant E. **Eichar** Can./R.83097 (US)/RCAF **BL967** VB -

Hit by wind gust on landing, bounced, stalled and undercarriage leg collapsed, Kirton-in-Lindsey. DBR. Eichar had been in the squadron since February and was killed three months later (see operational losses).

Note on the aircraft : TOC No.12 MU 19.02.42, issued No.133 Sqn 10.04.42, from No.601 Sqn.

28.07.42 P/O Ben P. **DeHaven** RAF No.116467 (US)/RAF **BL807** VB †

Crashed in unknown circumstances, but on a non-operational flight. DeHaven, an American from Kentucky, had been posted to the squadron the previous month.

Note on the aircraft : TOC No.39 MU 14.02.42, issued to No.133 Sqn 14.04.42, from No.601 Sqn.

19.09.42 P/O Seymour M. **Schatzberg** RAF No.118585 (US)/RAF **EP167** VA †

Collided, during a training flight, with another Spitfire and crashed at Scharndon Farm near Mayfield. Schatzberg, an American from New York, had arrived to the squadron only 11 days earlier.

Note on the aircraft : TOC No.9 MU 22.05.42, issued to No.133 Sqn 13.06.42. Was one of the few Mk.Vs which remained with the squadron for training duties after conversion onto the Mk.IX.

MAGISTER

26.07.42   P/O Gilbert I. OMENS   RAF No.108642   (US)/RAF   **N3929**   I   †

Engine cut during a communication flight and aircraft hit tree while force-landing near Guildford, Surrey. Omens was an American from Illinois.

Note on the aircraft : TOC No.5 MU 23.01.39, issued to No.133 Sqn 14.07.42. Served previously with No.609 Sqn.

Total: 15
including 14 combat aircraft

APPENDIX VII
Aircraft serial numbers matching with individual letters

MD-A
BM263 (*Spitfire V*)
BS313 (*Spitfire IX*)
MD-B
Z3335 (*Hurricane II*)
BS272 (*Spitfire IX*)
MD-C
BM260 (*Spitfire V*)
MD-D
BS137 (*Spitfire IX*)
MD-E
BL488 (*Spitfire V*)
MD-F
Z3828 (*Hurricane II*)
MD-G
P8191 (*Spitfire II*)
BL995 (*Spitfire V*)
MD-H

MD-I
BM353 (*Spitfire V*)
BS294 (*Spitfire IX*)
MD-J
MD-K
MD-L
MD-M
MD-N
BS143 (*Spitfire IX*)
MD-O
MD-P
MD-Q

MD-R
MD-S
BS296 (*Spitfire IX*)
MD-T
Z6919 (*Hurricane I*)
MD-U
Z3781 (*Hurricane II*)
EN951 (*Spitfire V*)
MD-V
BR640 (*Spitfire IX*)
MD-W
MD-X
MD-Y
Z3457 (*Hurricane II*)
MD-Z

APPENDIX VIII
LIST OF KNOWN PILOTS POSTED OR ATTACHED TO THE SQUADRON

RAF

W.A. **Arends**, RAF No.122280, USA
H.L. **Ayres**, RAF No.116157, USA
W.H. **Baker**, RAF No.108626, USA
C.S. **Barrell**, RAF No.102519, USA
C.E. **Bateman**, RAF No.89703, USA
R.N. **Beaty**, RAF No.115121, USA
J.L. **Bennett**, RAF No.102635, USA
E.H. **Bicksler**, RAF No.107781, USA
C.O. **Bodding**, RAF No.108628, USA
F.R. **Boyles**, RAF No.111571, USA
R.G. **Braley**, RAF No.120128, USA
R.V. **Brossmer**, RAF No.106352, USA
G.A. **Brown**, RAF No.39851
H.C. **Brown**, RAF No.103467, USA
G.R. **Bruce**, RAF No.67580, USA
C.A. **Cook**, RAF No.103476, USA
J.G. **Coxetter**, RAF No.104392, USA
S.H. **Crowe**, RAF No.67582, USA
B.P. **DeHaven**, RAF No.116467, USA
E. **Doorly**, RAF No.101458, USA
W.V. **Edwards**, RAF No.103477, USA
W.K. **Ford**, RAF No.111238, USA
T.A. **Gallo**, RAF No.100988, USA
D.S. **Gentile**, RAF No.112302, USA
L. **Gover**, RAF No.113986, USA
J.A. **Gray**, RAF No.108634, USA
D.D. **Gudmundsen**, RAF No.112295, USA
H.C. **Hain**, RAF No.100518, USA
F. **Hancock**, RAF No.113991, USA
M.E. **Jackson**, RAF No.100519, USA
H.A.S. **Johnstone**, RAF No.88723
C.C. **King**, RAF No.100521, USA
D.E. **Lambert**, RAF No.112282, USA
L.S. **Loomis**, RAF No.100522, USA
A.B. **Mamedoff**, RAF No.81621, USA
H.H. **McCall**, RAF No.67583, USA
C.W. **McColpin**, RAF No.61926, USA
C.E. **Meierhoff**, RAF No.100524, USA
G.H. **Middleton**, RAF No.112311, USA
E.L. **Miller**, RAF No.112304, USA
D.E. **Miner**, RAF No.100992, USA
J. **Mitchellweis**, RAF No.605376, USA
M.S. **Morris**, RAF No.102052, USA
R.S. **Mueller**, RAF No.100993, USA
D.D. **Nee**, RAF No.116156, USA
J.C. **Nelson**, RAF No.100525, USA
G.P. **Neville**, RAF No.115120, USA
G.I. **Omens**, RAF No.108642, USA
K.D. **Peterson**, RAF No.119030, USA
R.L. **Pewitt**, RAF No.100528, USA
L.T. **Ryerson**, RAF No.112285, USA
R.O. **Scarborough**, RAF No.65976, USA
S.M. **Schatzberg**, RAF No.118585, USA
G.W. **Scott**, RAF No.62257
F. **Scudday**, RAF No.61932, USA
W.C. **Slade**, RAF No.115520, USA
G.J. **Smart**, RAF No.112293, USA
D.D. **Smith**, RAF No.116464, USA
R.E. **Smith**, RAF No.116463, USA
W.G. **Soares**, RAF No.100532, USA
G.B. **Sperry**, RAF No.100533, USA
A.J. **Stephenseon**, RAF No.116958, USA
M.L. **Stepp**, RAF No.67579, USA
R.N. **Stout** Jr., RAF No.100531, USA
H.H. **Strickland**, RAF No.101461, USA
E.D. **Taylor**, RAF No.102053, USA
E.H. **Thomas**, RAF No.39138
W.R. **Wallace**, RAF No.103479, USA
J.W. **Warner**, RAF No.65977, USA
V.E. **Watkins**, RAF No.64868, USA
S.F. **Whedon**, RAF No.101462, USA
W.J. **White**, RAF No.100535, USA
R.L. **Wolfe**, RAF No.102518, USA
G.G. **Wright**, RAF No.112286, USA

RCAF

R.L. **Alexander**, Can./R.67881, USA
F.C. **Austin**, Can./R.58580, USA
D.J.M. **Blakeslee**, Can./J.4551, USA
G.C. **Daniel**, Can./J.15016, USA
G.E. **Eichar**, Can./J.15650, USA
D.R. **Florance**, Can./J.15193, USA
J.A. **Goodson**, Can./R.97032, USA
C.W. **Harp**, Can./J.15389, USA
R.D. **Hobert**, Can./R.97580, USA
K.K. **Kimbro**, Can./J.15082, USA
J.G. **Matthews**, Can./J.9471, USA
C.H. **Miley**, Can./J.15653, USA
G.E. **Mirsch**, Can./R.98263, USA
H.A. **Putnam**, Can./J.15079, USA
C.H. **Chesley**, Can./R.98048, USA
W.W. **Sobanski**, Can./R.54384, USA
W.C. **Wicker**, Can./R.74415, USA

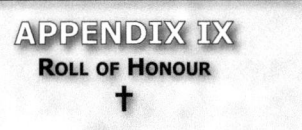

APPENDIX IX
ROLL OF HONOUR
✝

AIRCREW

Name	Service No	Rank	Age	Origin	Date	Serial
ARENDS, William Albert	RAF No.112280	P/O	24	(US)/RAF	20.06.42	EP168
BAKER, William Henry	RAF No.108626	F/O	22	(US)/RAF	26.09.42	BS446
BARRELL, Charles Sewall	RAF No.102519	P/O	29	(US)/RAF	27.09.41	Z3828
BRETTELL, Edward Gordon*	RAF No.61053	F/L	29	RAF	31.03.44	BS313
BROWN, Hugh Card	RAF No.103467	P/O	21	(US)/RAF	16.03.42	X4353
BRUCE, George Russell	RAF No.67580	P/O	27	(US)/RAF	23.10.41	Z3649
COXETTER, James Geiger	RAF No.104392	P/O	23	(US)/RAF	27.10.41	Z3182
DeHAVEN, Ben Perry	RAF No.116467	P/O	25	(US)/RAF	28.07.42	BL807
EICHAR, Grant Eugene	Can./J.15650	P/O	27	(US)/RCAF	31.07.42	BM646
FLORANCE, David Ray	Can./J.15193	P/O	22	(US)/RCAF	19.05.42	AD502
FORD, William Kenneth	RAF No.111238	P/O	22	(US)/RAF	31.05.42	BL961
GUDMUNDSEN, Dick D.	RAF No.112295	P/O	26	(US)/RAF	06.09.42	BS292
HANCOCK, Fletcher	RAF No.113991	P/O	22	(US)/RAF	05.06.42	BM260
HARP, Carter Woodruff	Can./J.15389	P/O	33	(US)/RCAF	31.07.42	BL982
KING, Coburn Clark	RAF No.100521	F/L	33	(US)/RAF	31.07.42	BL938
MORRIS, Moran Scott	RAF No.102052	P/O	24	(US)/RAF	31.05.42	BL996
MAMEDORFF, Andrew B.	RAF No.81621	F/L	30	(US)/RAF	08.10.41	Z3781
McCALL, Hugh Harrison	RAF No.67583	P/O	24	(US)/RAF	08.10.41	Z3677
NEVILLE, Gene Parks	RAF No.115120	P/O	24	(US)/RAF	26.09.42	BS140
OMENS, Gilbert Inland	RAF No.108642	P/O	24	(US)/RAF	26.07.42	N3929
PEWITT, Robert Lewis	RAF No.100528	P/O	22	(US)/RAF	19.05.42	BL988
RYERSON, Leonard Thomas	RAF No.112285	P/O	31	(US)/RAF	26.09.42	BS275
SCHATZBERG, Seymour Morton	RAF No.118585	P/O	23	(US)/RAF	19.09.42	EP167
SMITH, Dennis David	RAF No.116464	P/O	22	(US)/RAF	26.09.42	BS137
SOARES, Walter Gordon	RAF No.100532	P/O	22	(US)/RAF	27.09.41	Z3335
STOUT, Roy Neal Jr.	RAF No.100531	P/O	24	(US)/RAF	08.10.41	Z3253
WHEDON, Samuel Fisk	RAF No.100531	P/O	21	(US)/RAF	03.04.42	P8438
WHITE, William Joseph	RAF No.100535	P/O	21	(US)/RAF	08.10.41	Z3457
WICKER, Walter Charles	Can./R.74415	F/Sgt	20	(US)/RCAF	27.04.42	BM264

*Excecuted while a PoW during the 'Great Escape'.

Total: 29

United Kingdom: 1
United States: 28

GROUNDCREW
NONE

After debuting on Hurricane Mk.IIs and Spitfire Mk.IIs, No.133 Squadron converted to the Spitfire Mk.V, the predominant model in use by Fighter Command in 1942 and the type it flew until transferring to the USAAF in September 1942. Even after updating to the Spitfire Mk.IX, the squadron kept a couple of Spitfire Mk.Vs for training duties.
Top: BM260/MD-C, which was lost on 5 June 1942, and below, the CO's aircraft MD-A/BM263. Note the wheels painted with the RAF roundel and also the positioning of the Squadron Leader pennant under the nose, an unusual place.

CO's aircraft MD-A/BM263 taken from another angle.

Because No.133 (Eagle) Squadron had a short operational life, it did not see the emergence of many promising or successful pilots. However, the Squadron could count on many American experienced pilots, like 'Red' McColpin (left) who arrived in January 1942 from No. 71 (Eagle) Squadron to lead B Flight and would eventually take over the squadron in September. He will continue his career with the USAAF retiring as a Major General in 1968.

F/L Don Blakeslee (bottom left) was one of the few exceptions, although he had previously served with two Canadian squadrons, Nos.411 and 401, before joining the third Eagle squadron. But definitely, he played a central role in the existence of the Squadron. He survived the war and continued to serve with the USAAF until 1965.

Below right, Andrew Mamedorff, one of the very first 'Eagle' pilots who joined No. 71 Squadron on formation in 1940 and a veteran of the Battle of Britain. He had gained a great experience and was chosen to become one of the Flight Commander when the 133 was formed. Sadly he was killed in a flying accident one month later.

No.133 (Eagle) Squadron in June 1942:

Standing, from left to right : P/O Leonard T. Ryerson from New Hampshire (†26.09.42), P/O George H. Middleton from Iowa (PoW 26.09.42), P/O Richard N. Beaty from New York, F/O Ervin L. Miller from Oklahoma, P/O Dick D. Gudmundsen from Idaho (†06.09.42), P/O Donald E. Lambert from California, P/O Dominic S. Gentile from Ohio, P/O J.M. Emerson (Intelligence Officer), F/O F.J.S. Chapman (Doctor), F/O D.G. Stavely-Dick (Adjutant), F/Sgt Grant E. Eichar from Iowa (†31.07.42), F/Sgt Chesley H. Robertson from Mississippi.

Front row, from left to right : P/O Carter W. Harp from Alabama (†31.07.42), P/O William A. Arends from North Dakota (†20.06.42), P/O Gilbert I. Omens from Illinois (†26.07.42), P/O Edwin D. Taylor from Oklahoma, F/L Coburn C. King from Missouri (†31.07.42), S/L Eric H. Thomas, F/L Donald J.M. Blakeslee from Ohio, P/O George B. Sperry from California (PoW 26.09.42), P/O Eric Doorly from New Jersey, P/O Karl K. Kimbro from Mississippi, P/O William H. Baker from Texas (†26.09.42).

The formation of the third Eagle squadron was made possible with the arrival of new pilots fresh graduates from summer 1941. Top left, P/O William R. Wallace from California is seen here in Hurricane Mk.IIB MD-G, believed to be Z3649, an aircraft that suffered a Cat.B accident on 23 October 1941. He had arrived one week before and was posted out in February 1942 as an instructor at No. 59 OTU. He could not stay with the squadron because of an old shoulder wound and became unfit for fighter duties. He eventually transferred to the USAAF in September 1943.
Top right, Richard 'Dixie' Alexander from Illinois was posted in when Wallace left and transferred in September 1942. He ended the war as a PoW after being shot down on 30 May 1944.
Below left, Carl 'Spike' Miley from Ohio arrived at the same time in February 1942 and transferred as well in September 1942. He survived the war and left the Air Force shortly after the war.
Below right, LeRoy Gover from Colorado was him, a late arrival, in August 1942. He transferred and left the Air Force shortly after the war.

Without a doubt Dominic 'Don' Gentile has been one of the most outstanding pilots who joined No.133 Sqn. Born in Ohio he enlisted in the RAF in 1941 and after his commission, he sailed from Halifax (Canada) to the United Kingdom in December that year. There, he learned to fly Spitfires and he reported to the Squadron early in June 1942. He distinguished himself during Operation 'Jubilee', during which he claimed two confirmed victories. The following month, he transferred to the US Army Air Force and continued to fly with the 4th FG flying Spitfires then P-47 Thunderbolts. But what will make Gentile famous began when he made the transition from the P-47 to the P-51 Mustang. Between December 1943 and April 1944, he managed to claim 22 German aircraft as destroyed to become one the top aces of the USAAF. In April 1944 he was sent back to the USA and never flew in operations again. He left the Army in 1946 but soon reentered the new US Air Force in December 1947. Sadly he was killed on 28 January 1951 during a routine training flight on a T-33 (s/n 49-0905).

Summary of the operational activity
No.133 (Eagle) Squadron

A/C types	First sortie	Last sortie	Total sorties	Tot Sub-type	Lost Ops	Lost Acc	A/C lost	Claims	V-1	Pilot †	PoWs	Eva.
Hurricane II	29.09.41	15.12.41	96	96	1	7	8	-	-	8	-	-
Spitfire II	08.11.41	24.12.41	105	105	-	1	1	-	-	-	1	-
Spitfire V	06.01.42	20.08.42	1,740	1,740	12	6	18	21.5	-	14	-	-
Spitfire IX	04.09.42	26.09.42	36	36	14	-	14	1.0	-	5	6	2
Others												
Magister	-	-	-	-	-	1	1	-	-	1	-	-
Other causes	-	-	-	-	-	-	-	-	-	1	-	-
Compilation	29.09.41	26.09.42	1,978		27	15	42	22.5	-	29	7	2

Main Awards

DSO: -
DFC: 3
DFM: -

Points of interest:
- Last of the three squadrons formed with American volunteers.
- One of the few squadrons fully equipped with Spitfire Mk.VA.
- One of the first squadrons to operate Spitfire Mk.IXs.
- Sustained one of the heavier losses in a single mission for a Fighter Command squadron.

Unsolved mystery:
None

Statistics:
- Lost one aircraft every 73 sorties [Hurricane I: 96, Spitfire II: -, Spitfire V: 145, Spitfire IX: 2.6]
- 35.7 % of the combat aircraft losses occurred during non operational flights.

BADGE
On a hurt semee of mullets an eagle displayed.

The eagle and stars in the badge commemorates the squadron's association with the U.S.A.

MOTTO
LET US TO THE BATTLE

Authority: King George VI, September 1942

Supermarine Spitfire Mk.VB BM263, Squadron Leader Eric H. Thomas (RAF), Kirton-in-Lindsey, Spring 1942.
This aircraft was presented by the people of York, which was painted on the right side of the aircraft. It was taken on charge on 23 March 1942 and was issued to No.133 Sqn on the following 12 April to become the CO's mount for the next few weeks with a personal artwork 'MINES A BITTER' which was also painted under the cockpit with also as Squadron Leader pennant under the nose. Eric Thomas took command of the Biggin Hill and Hornchurch Wing between August and December 1942 when he completed his tour. He never came back to the front-line units and was eventually released from service in September 1944 due to ill-health problem, leaving the RAF with a DSO, DFC and Bar, five confirmed victories, one being shared.
Note that the wheels were also painted with the RAF roundels (see photo page 16.)

Supermarine Spitfire Mk.IXB BS294, Pilot Officer Dennis D. Smith (USA), Great Samford, 26 September 1942.
No.133 Squadron became one of the first Fighter Command units to receive the Mk.IX version of the Spitfire. BS294 was one of the first produced, converted from a Mk.V as can attest the top of the engine cowling. This aircraft first flew on 11 August 1942 and issued to No.133 Sqn two days later. This aircraft was lost during the fateful day of 26 September which became of one the heavier losses sustained by Fighter Command units during a single mission. Dennis D. Smith was killed in that aircraft. No.133 Sqn has been selected to be the first of the three Eagle squadrons to fly with the Mk.IX, but this blow prevented this plan to become a reality and the 133 Sqn was converted back to the older Mk.V just before to be transferred to the USAAF. This was the second severe blow sustained by No.133 Squadron after the loss of four pilots the and planes the previous year during a ferry flight on 8 October 1941.

www.ingramcontent.com/pod-product-compliance
Lightning Source LLC
Chambersburg PA
CBHW041542040426
42446CB00002B/207